THE 10

COOLEST ISLANDS
IN THE UNITED STATES

Stephanie Payne

Series Editor
Mark Pearcy

Contents

9

14

20

An Adventure in Your Own Backyard

When you think about islands, you might think about tropical vacation spots, such as Jamaica or the Bahamas. Or maybe an island nation, such as Japan or England, comes to mind.

But did you know that there are beautiful and interesting islands in your own backyard? People from around the world come to explore the islands of the United States every year.

Islands can have histories that are very different from those of mainland areas. Landscapes, climates, plants, and animals can differ from island to island as well. And each island can have its own culture and traditions.

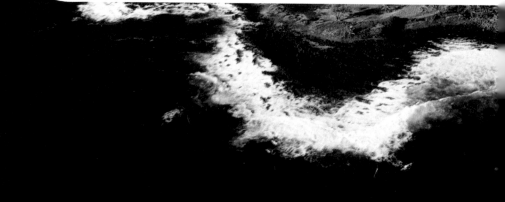

In this book, we rank what we think are the ten most interesting islands in the United States. When choosing and ranking the islands, we thought about the following criteria:

- Does it have interesting geographical features?

- Did any important historical events take place on the island?

- Do many people visit the island?

- Does the island have any unique plants or animals?

As you read this book, ask yourself:

What is the coolest island in the United States?

⑩ Chincoteague Island

Cool Factor: Visitors can come to this island to see horses go for a swim.

Chincoteague Island is located off the coast of Virginia. It is known for giving its name to a breed of horse called the Chincoteague pony. The island was made famous by author Marguerite Henry, who wrote a book called *Misty of Chincoteague* in 1947. The book was inspired by the Chincoteague pony. In 1961, a film based on the book was filmed on Chincoteague Island.

Chincoteague ponies continue to draw people to the island. Tourists come especially for the **annual** Pony Swim. In this event, Chincoteague ponies swim between Chincoteague Island and nearby Assateague Island. The event raises money for the local fire department, which takes care of the horses.

Chincoteague Island's very popular Pony Swim and relaxed way of life make it a unique place.

THE EXPERT SAYS

"[The Pony Swim is] the one time of year when things can get really hectic on the island — though many people say the event is so cool that it's worth dealing with the crowds."

— Stacey Sykes, travel writer, 2014

9 Nantucket

Cool Factor: Nantucket was once the whaling capital of the world.

Nantucket is a small island off the coast of Cape Cod, Massachusetts. Nantucket is known as a beach town that people escape to during the summer. But it also has a long history.

Nantucket was settled in 1659. During the early years of settlement, American Indians and settlers caught whales for blubber. The fat of the whales could be turned into oil, which made whale fat very valuable. The island eventually gained a **reputation** as the whaling capital of the world.

However, this reputation came to an end in 1846. A large fire tore through the town, destroying the harbor and hundreds of buildings. In the 1870s, Nantucket began to be rebuilt. The new look of the town was designed to attract tourists.

With its history as an early settlement and its survivor spirit, Nantucket is an important part of the United States.

THE EXPERT SAYS

"Now one of the most popular and attractive destinations in the world ... Nantucket [is] unparalleled in the distinction of its architecture and its historical ambience."

— Elizabeth Oldham, writer, 2000

8 Galveston

Cool Factor: This island was once the largest city in Texas.

Galveston, Texas, is an island in the Gulf of Mexico. It was an important port city during the 1800s, and by the late 1800s, it had the largest population in Texas.

In 1900, a hurricane tore through the island. It is estimated that at least 6,000 people lost their lives. This hurricane is still considered the deadliest natural disaster in U.S. history. Afterward, a large **seawall** was constructed to protect the island from another natural disaster.

Despite the damage from the hurricane, many historic homes and sites still remain on Galveston. The historic district of the island has some of the most well-**preserved** nineteenth-century homes in the country.

Although Galveston suffered the worst natural disaster the country has ever seen, it has preserved its history and become a place that people love to visit.

THE EXPERT SAYS

"Galveston is a Texas gem. With more than 6 million visitors a year, it has a warm island feel and is brimming with things to do."

— Joy Sewing, journalist, 2017

The Galveston Island Historic Pleasure Pier is a popular attraction.

7 U.S. Virgin Islands

Cool Factor: These islands are a recent addition to the United States.

The U.S. Virgin Islands are located in the Caribbean. They include the islands of St. Croix, St. John, and St. Thomas. Together, the islands are a territory of the United States.

It is believed that Christopher Columbus, in the late 1500s, was the first European to land on the islands. There are rumors that other famous captains visited the islands, too. It has been said that one of the castles on St. Thomas once belonged to the **infamous** pirate Blackbeard.

The United States bought the islands from Denmark in 1917. Today, the U.S. Virgin Islands receive nearly three million visitors each year.

Even though they are fairly new to the United States, the U.S. Virgin Islands have a long history that every American can be interested in exploring.

THE EXPERT SAYS

"[The U.S. Virgin Islands are] a world full of **intrigue** and drama, history and promise ..."

— Cynthia Moulton, biologist, 2016

6 Florida Keys

Cool Factor: The Florida Keys have the only living coral reef in the continental United States.

The Florida Keys are a series of islands. The Keys stretch for 220 miles south of Florida. They include the regions of Key Largo, Islamorada, Marathon, the Lower Keys, and Key West. The unique culture of the Keys blends American and Caribbean ways of life.

While island life in the Keys pulls in many visitors, what is most interesting about the Keys lies under the water. The Keys are home to the only living coral reef in the continental United States.

HOW COOL IS THAT?

Military ships and other items were placed at the bottom of the ocean. They were put there so that they could become artificial reefs. The old ships and equipment help to **cultivate** the coral reefs.

A wide variety of fish species can be found among the reefs. But fish are not all that divers find — the reefs are peppered with old shipwrecks. Treasure hunters and marine life fans flock to the Keys to explore what lies under the water. Some have even found lost treasures during their dives.

Thanks to their unique underwater scenes, the Florida Keys are unlike anywhere else in the United States.

THE EXPERT SAYS

"From the visitors who fill dive charters ... to the local fishing industry's catches ... nearly everything in the Florida Keys is tied in some way to the reefs."

— Chris Mooney, journalist, 2017

⑤ Puerto Rico

Cool Factor: The oldest city under U.S. control, San Juan, is found on this island.

Puerto Rico is a Caribbean island that is also a territory of the United States. The island was surrendered by Spain to the United States in 1898 after the Spanish-American War. Reminders of Puerto Rico's Spanish history can still be seen throughout the island.

Spanish history can be seen most **prominently** in an area called Old San Juan. This is a section of the capital city, San Juan. Old San Juan has some of the most beautiful historic buildings in the Caribbean. San Juan was founded in 1521.

HOW COOL IS THAT?

The only tropical rain forest in the United States national forest system is located in Puerto Rico. It is called El Yunque.

Puerto Rico also boasts sandy beaches, scenic mountains, and dense forests. Several different **ecosystems** exist on the island, including seagrass beds, coral reefs, and tropical rain forests.

Puerto Rico has been part of the United States for only a little more than 100 years. However, it is home to the oldest buildings in the country, and it has a history and a culture all its own. Puerto Rico is truly a unique part of the United States.

THE EXPERT SAYS

"While the beach is nice, it's even nicer that if you need a break, there's actually something else to do. Puerto Rico's forts and cathedrals date back to the 16th century, when Spain ruled the island."

— Paula Froelich, journalist, 2015

El Morro, a castle in San Juan

4 Ellis Island

Cool Factor: Nearly 40 percent of Americans have ancestors who came to the country through Ellis Island.

Ellis Island is a small island with a big history. It is located in the water between New York and New Jersey. The island served as a center for new immigrants from 1892 to 1954. Ellis Island was the first immigration center to be run by the government of the United States. Previously, each state had handled immigration on its own.

HOW COOL IS THAT?

The location of Ellis Island has caused **controversy** over the years. The island is located in Upper New York Bay. The waters technically belong to New Jersey, but at one point, the state of New York believed the island belonged to it. In 1834, an agreement was reached, and now both states own areas of the island.

Millions of people passed through Ellis Island while it was an immigration center. Today, three million people visit the island every year to see the site that many of their ancestors passed through on their journeys to begin new lives in the United States. The Ellis Island National Museum of Immigration is located on the island. At the museum, people can read through arrival records to get a glimpse of their family history.

Ellis Island was the gateway to the United States for millions of future Americans. It is not only an island but a **symbol** of what makes the country the **multicultural** place it is.

THE EXPERT SAYS

"Approximately 40 percent of the United States population is descended from immigrants who passed through Ellis Island."

— Maeve McDermott, writer, 2017

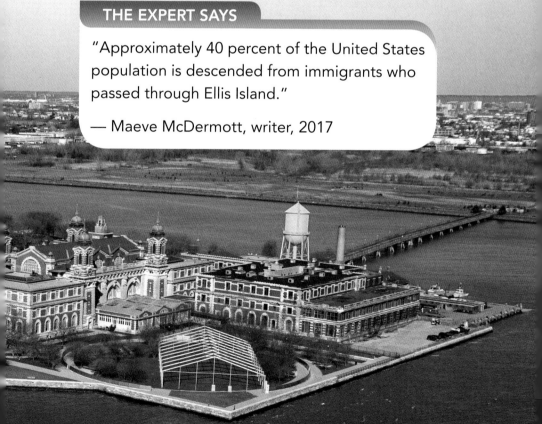

③ Alcatraz Island

Cool Factor: This little island has housed some of the most infamous criminals in U.S. history.

Many people will know Alcatraz from movies or books that highlight its dark history as a prison. Alcatraz is an island located just off the coast of San Francisco. It was a military prison before it became the federal prison that it is most famous for being. Prisoners who were especially dangerous or who were likely to escape lived behind the bars of the prison that was also known as "The Rock." They were sent to Alcatraz because it was believed to be the most secure prison in the United States.

The water surrounding Alcatraz is one of the reasons the island was chosen as a prison site. The currents in the water are very strong. It was believed that escapees would be unable to swim against them.

Alcatraz was active as a prison from 1934 to 1963. During this time, there were 14 attempted escapes involving 36 prisoners. However, no one is believed to have ever escaped from Alcatraz successfully.

HOW COOL IS THAT?

The first lighthouse on the West Coast of the United States was built on Alcatraz.

Alcatraz was intimidating enough to hold some of the worst criminals in U.S. history. The island shows us how the location of a place can be enough to tame the wildest natures.

THE EXPERT SAYS

"Although this was viewed by the public as a notorious place which held 'the worst of the worst,' living on the island was a unique ... experience."

— Jim Albright, former Alcatraz prison guard

② Manhattan

Cool Factor: This island is home to some of the most famous landmarks in the United States.

The Empire State Building. Broadway. Central Park. Times Square. These are some of the most well-known places in the United States. And they are all found on one island: Manhattan.

Manhattan is a **borough** of New York City. It has a population of 1.6 million people, who all live within 22 square miles. With so many people living in so small a space, the island can be very busy.

HOW COOL IS THAT?

Many people think of the bright lights of Times Square when they think of Manhattan. However, a huge area of green space has been preserved on the island. This is Central Park. The park provides locals and visitors a rest from the concrete jungle. Many animal species live in the park, and it also houses its very own zoo.

Seals can be seen at the Central Park Zoo.

Besides its famous landmarks, Manhattan is home to a rich history and culture. The island was one of the first places to be settled by European people.

Many of the people who were on their way to Ellis Island's immigration center had to dock in Manhattan at one point. Manhattan has become a cultural hot spot largely because of its multicultural population. The people make Manhattan what it is today.

From the earliest days of settlement to the present, Manhattan has always been a central part of U.S. culture and history.

THE EXPERT SAYS

"During the workday, the population [of Manhattan] doubles."

— Amy O'Leary, journalist, 2012

1 Hawaii

Cool Factor: These islands were created from volcanic eruptions.

The state of Hawaii is made up of a number of islands. Each of these islands was formed at a different time. This is because they were all formed by various volcanic eruptions.

In fact, one of the volcanoes in Hawaii is erupting to this day. This is the Kīlauea volcano, and it has been erupting constantly since 1983. It is the most active volcano in the world.

HOW COOL IS THAT?

There are many species of plants and animals that exist only on the Hawaiian islands. This fact has puzzled scientists for years. Scientists are not always able to trace the species on the islands back to other plants or animals found elsewhere in the world.

The nene is the state bird of Hawaii. It is found only on the islands.

In 2015, more than eight million tourists visited the Hawaiian islands. The islands are full of interesting features, including beaches with red, black, and green sand and mountain ranges.

But Hawaii is not just home to lush forests and beautiful beaches. One of the most significant events in U.S. history happened in Hawaii. Japan attacked the U.S. naval base at Pearl Harbor, Hawaii, in 1941. This event caused the United States to enter World War II. Today, there is a visitor center at Pearl Harbor. Millions of people visit this historic site every year.

In addition to active volcanoes and unique plants and animals, Hawaii's warm climate, excellent beaches, and friendly locals continue to attract visitors. In Hawaii, people can see things they will see nowhere else in the United States.

USS *Arizona* Memorial

THE EXPERT SAYS

"Whenever I land [in Hawaii], I feel as though I've gone back in time."

— Kaui Hart Hemmings, author, 2007

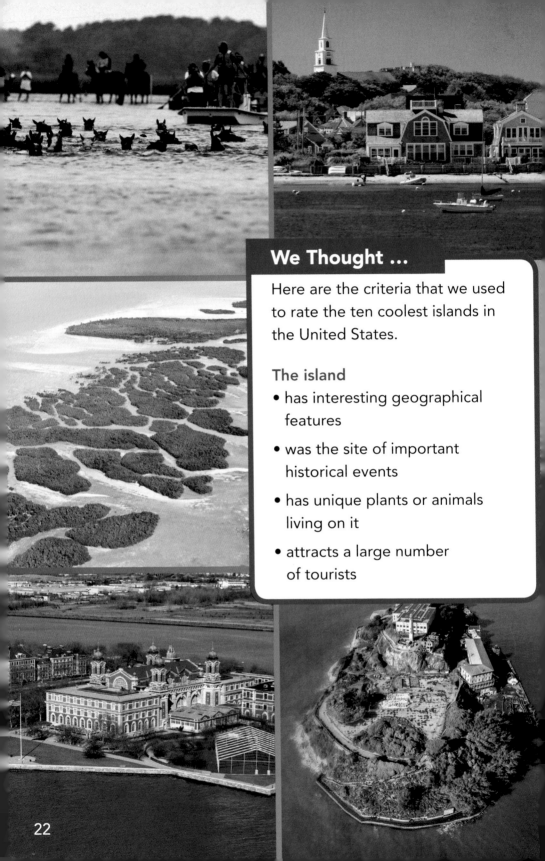

We Thought ...

Here are the criteria that we used to rate the ten coolest islands in the United States.

The island
- has interesting geographical features
- was the site of important historical events
- has unique plants or animals living on it
- attracts a large number of tourists

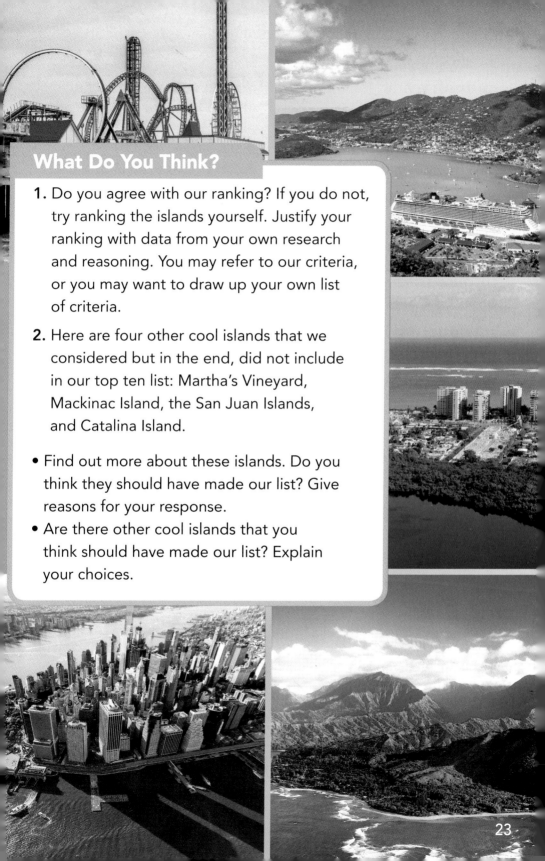

What Do You Think?

1. Do you agree with our ranking? If you do not, try ranking the islands yourself. Justify your ranking with data from your own research and reasoning. You may refer to our criteria, or you may want to draw up your own list of criteria.

2. Here are four other cool islands that we considered but in the end, did not include in our top ten list: Martha's Vineyard, Mackinac Island, the San Juan Islands, and Catalina Island.

- Find out more about these islands. Do you think they should have made our list? Give reasons for your response.
- Are there other cool islands that you think should have made our list? Explain your choices.

GLOSSARY

annual: yearly

borough: a section of a city

controversy: strong disagreement

cultivate: to help to grow

ecosystems: groups of living things and their surroundings

infamous: known for something negative

intrigue: a mysterious feature

multicultural: made up of many cultures

preserved: kept intact or in good condition

prominently: noticeably

reputation: the character of something as seen by other people

seawall: a wall built to protect a shoreline

symbol: a thing that can stand for or represent something else

INDEX